LADY OF THE LINES

How Maria Reiche
Saved the Nazca Lines
by Sweeping the Desert

Michaela MacColl

Illustrated by
Elisa Chavarri

ASTRA YOUNG READERS
AN IMPRINT OF ASTRA BOOKS FOR YOUNG READERS
New York

In Peru, an ancient civilization scratched gigantic figures—
- condor
- monkey
- pelican
- whale—

into the desert floor.
And mile after mile of perfectly straight lines.

Over centuries, sand and dust gradually filled the shallow grooves.

Only faint traces remained.

Pilots reported mysterious lines—but no one bothered to investigate.

Not until Maria Reiche came to sweep the desert.

Maria was born in 1903 in Dresden, Germany. As a girl she studied widely: languages, geology, math, and astronomy. She conducted scientific experiments during the day and stargazed at night.

Curiosity propelled Maria six thousand miles away from home—all the way to Peru, where she was greeted by a quadruple rainbow. A good omen.

Maria loved everything about Peru, especially the ancient culture of the Incas. She explored ruins in the rugged Andes Mountains and learned Quechua, the Incan language.

Peru had gifted Maria so much joy, she wished she could do something in return. Something important.

Her chance came in 1941 when she met Dr. Paul Kosok, an American anthropologist.

"The Peruvian earth has put its spell on me."

Dr. Kosok spread aerial photographs of the Nazca desert on a table. The Lines whispered so many questions that Maria longed to answer:

Who drew such wonders?
Why did they draw pictures in the sand?
How had the Lines lasted so long?

Dr. Kosok thought the Lines might be an ancient star chart and wanted to hire someone to investigate. Someone who was:
- good at math,
- interested in past civilizations,
- knowledgeable about astronomy,
- unafraid to live in the harsh desert, and
- willing to work for peanuts.

"You cannot predict when you will meet your destiny, but you know when it happens."

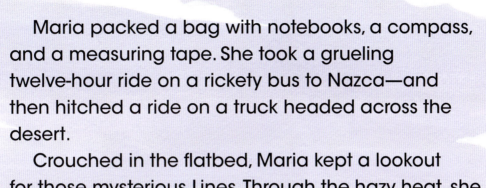

Maria packed a bag with notebooks, a compass, and a measuring tape. She took a grueling twelve-hour ride on a rickety bus to Nazca—and then hitched a ride on a truck headed across the desert.

Crouched in the flatbed, Maria kept a lookout for those mysterious Lines. Through the hazy heat, she spied . . . something in the sand. A line?

Maria banged on the rear window. STOP!

Alone in the desert, Maria felt instantly at home and set off to investigate.

"For many it is too desolate and forlorn. But for me it is my land. I feel as one with the vast sky, the dark rocky ground, the enormous plateau where a human gets lost like a small invisible dot in the distance."

But the line she'd seen had vanished!
Maria searched and searched.
Her head ached from squinting at the horizon.
And her shirt was soaked with sweat.
A line couldn't just disappear.

At last, Maria stumbled into a groove filled with loose dirt and pebbles.

Her eyes could just trace its path, straight and true, across the desert.

Maria knelt. Her hands trembling, she brushed aside the pebbles to find yellow clay underneath.

"When you set yourself an objective, you must insist, persist, even up to exhaustion."

Like chalk on a blackboard, the pale line contrasted with the darker stones of the desert.

Suddenly it was clear why no one knew about the Lines. From above one could see a faint outline where the line had been carved, but from the ground, the Lines were almost invisible.

The answers were hidden under centuries of accumulated pebbles and dust!

"The lines look as if they were traced by giants with kilometric rulers."

Maria bought all the brooms Dr. Kosok's money could buy. So many that the townspeople called her a bruja, a witch. With the little money she had left, she purchased sweet potatoes to eat for breakfast, lunch, and dinner.

Every morning she:
> woke at 5:00 AM to beat the sun,
> wrapped her head in a wet cloth to keep cool,
> slipped on padded flip-flops (to protect the fragile Lines), and
> hiked across the desert to sweep her latest line.

Painstaking. Backbreaking. Sun burning her skin to leather. Her fascination with the Lines made every hardship worthwhile.

As she swept and cataloged each perfectly straight line, she remembered Kosok's photos. Especially the one of a curved line, like a wing buried in the sand.

A curved line invited Maria to follow. The line looped and looped again, never crossing itself.

Quick as a hummingbird's wings, Maria swept. She stopped only to record the line's arc and direction. Hour after hour until she ended up not far from where she began.

That night, using her detailed notes, Maria sketched the shape of her journey.

Not a bird.
Not a plant.
Not a person . . .

A SPIDER!
 A spider as big as four city buses laid end to end. An enormous, beautiful spider made from one single line.
 After years of sweeping, a menagerie sprouted from the pages of Maria's notebook.
 A monkey as big as a soccer field.
 A condor as long as a submarine.
 A whale whose mouth could swallow a blimp.
 But from the ground, Maria could only see a tiny portion of each figure. A tail here, a beak there.

"How was it possible to imprint on the ground the shape of a bird so big that if you step on the tip of one of its wings, it is not possible to know where you can find the head, legs, or tail?"

Maria had to go higher. So she:
　　strapped on wooden stilts,
　　perched on the hood of a car and
　　balanced atop a seven-foot ladder.
Still not high enough.
　　An airplane traveled too fast and too high for detailed photographs.
　　Maria fretted and fumed. Until one day a noisy helicopter buzzed over her head.

"Flying is the only way you can see the full beauty of the lines."

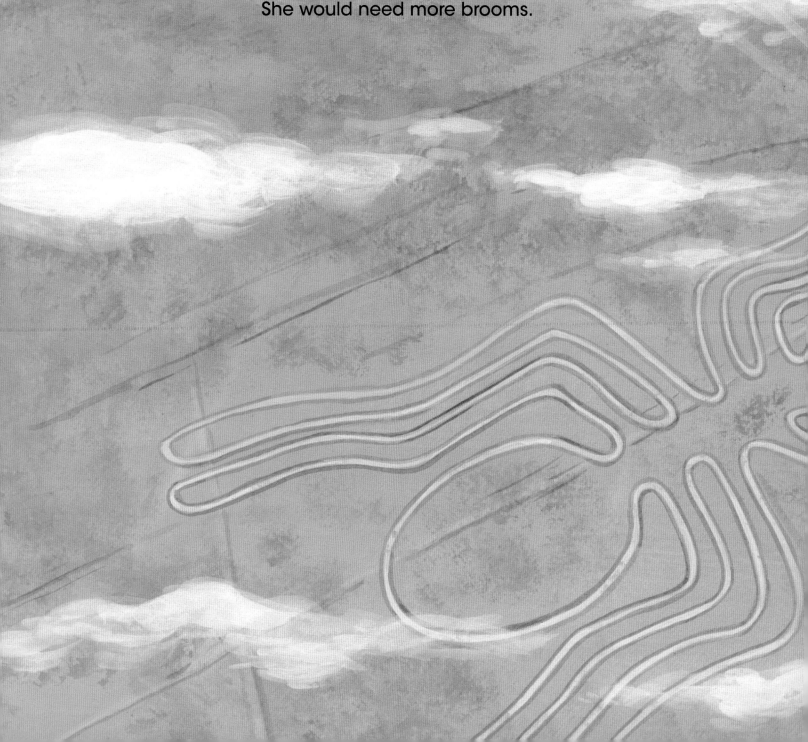

Maria tied herself to the landing skids. The ropes cut into her body and dust swirled into her eyes. But then she spotted her spider from the air. An entire glorious, gigantic arachnid!

She snapped picture after picture. Enough to map the entire desert.

When she developed her film, she saw every figure she had uncovered. But, even better, there were still others to discover.

She would need more brooms.

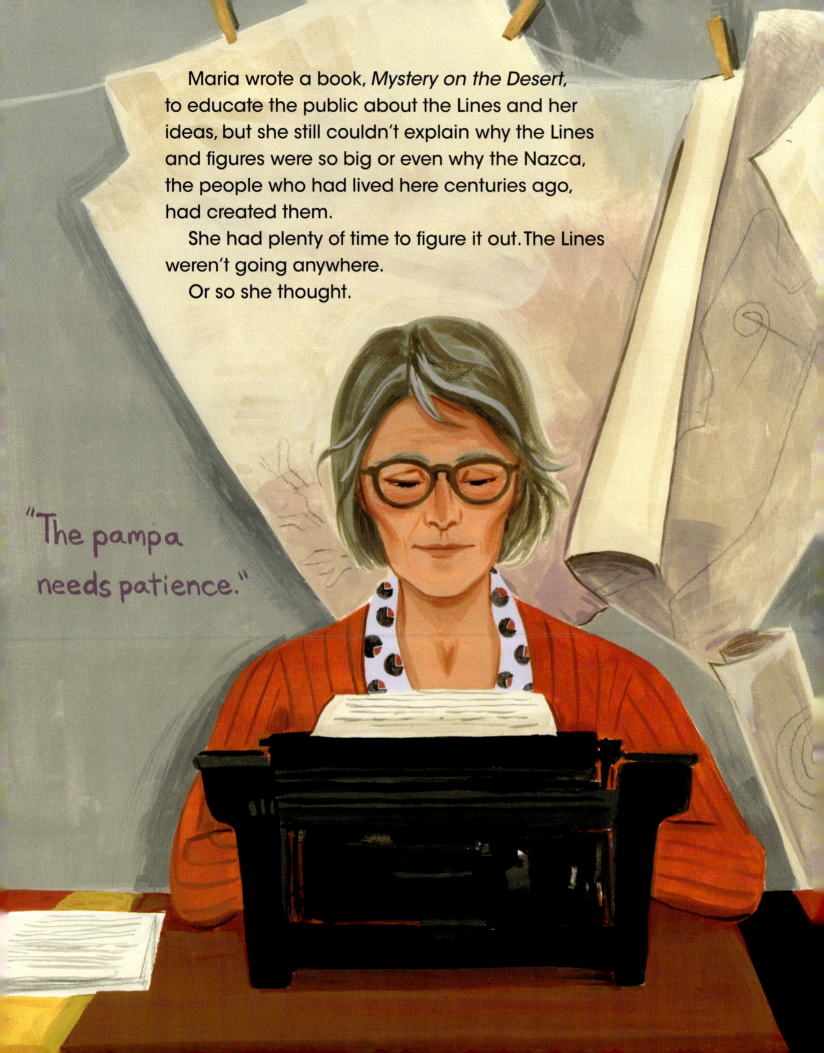

Maria wrote a book, *Mystery on the Desert*, to educate the public about the Lines and her ideas, but she still couldn't explain why the Lines and figures were so big or even why the Nazca, the people who had lived here centuries ago, had created them.

She had plenty of time to figure it out. The Lines weren't going anywhere.

Or so she thought.

"The pampa needs patience."

Maria woke to trucks careening across the desert, crushing lines under their tires. Wealthy farmers planned to irrigate the desert to grow cotton.

Maria protested: flooding would wash away the Lines forever! The only reason the Lines were still here was because the pampa, the local word for the desert, was one of the driest places on Earth.

The farmers had the power and the votes in the Peruvian Congress.

The Lines only had Maria.

Maria gathered her photographs and maps and set out to change minds.

She lobbied local politicians, gave speeches, and called in favors.

She got nowhere.

Then, using her connections in Germany and America, she convinced the international press that this was a BIG story.

Articles appeared all over the world. As the Peruvian people learned about the Lines, they called for them to be preserved. Maria was invited to address the Peruvian Congress.

The irrigation project was cancelled.

Victorious but exhausted, Maria couldn't wait to return to the desert.

Only to find a new problem.

"Nazca is unique in the world."

Tourists swarmed the pampa, carelessly trampling the fragile Lines. Maria chased them away, but she couldn't be everywhere all the time. She hired guards to patrol on motorbikes, but the desert was just too big.

What if she built a tower along the highway so tourists could see the Lines without damaging them? The government said a tower was too expensive. Again, Maria negotiated. She offered to pay for it herself, using the profits from her book. Her only condition? That admission be free to the public because the Lines belonged to everyone.

She had to plead her case all the way to the president of Peru, but Maria won. The tower was built. The Lines were safe again.

But for how long?

Decades of toiling in the desert had wrecked Maria's health. Nearly blind and in a wheelchair, she had to give up her sweeping. From a hotel room in Nazca, she continued her work using her notebooks.

But she wasn't alone.

Archaeologists from around the world came to study the Lines. Their first stop was always to meet with Maria, the expert.

Maria still believed that the Lines were a star chart and the figures represented constellations, but others had different ideas. Were they alien runways? Or meditation paths? Did they point to water?

Maria enjoyed the mystery. "If everything were clear, I would lose interest," she said.

Maria lived long enough to see the United Nations name the Nazca Lines a UNESCO World Heritage Site in 1994. The whole world would protect the Lines now, not just Maria Reiche and her brooms.

Maybe someday someone will figure out what the Lines mean.

Maybe you will.

Maria Reiche saved them for you.

A Word from the Author

I admire women like Maria Reiche who are smart, determined, brave, and curious. But even after all my research, Maria is still an enigma to me. What kind of woman spends 45 years sweeping the desert? Who chooses to live on nuts and cheap vegetables, without electricity or running water? Once Maria discovered her life's passion at age thirty-eight, nothing could stop her from pursuing it. At the end of her life, Maria acknowledged that she would never know why the Nazca carved lines in the sand. Far from being disappointed, she decided that to know everything would be boring.

I would never make the choices she did. And yet, I understand her drive to know more. My own research fills my days and thoughts. I wake in the middle of the night with ideas to better tell my stories. I too love my work. I believe Maria had a satisfying and happy life, doing something meaningful. What more could anyone ask for?

Inspired as I am by Maria's passion, I still don't completely understand her. Maria would say the mystery is the fun part.

Maria Reiche

Nothing in Maria's childhood in Dresden, Germany, hinted at the extraordinary life she would live. She grew up visiting lush gardens and traditional museums. At school she studied a variety of subjects, but then drifted between temporary, unsatisfying jobs. She wanted to do more, but what?

At age twenty-nine, on a whim, she took a job as a nanny in Peru. Peru would be her home for the rest of her life. She still did odd jobs: unwrapping mummies at the museum, massage therapy, teaching math, and baby-sitting. She also translated scientific papers. That's how she met the anthropologist Dr. Paul Kosok, who first showed Maria the Lines. To her, it seemed as if everything in her life had prepared her for this "fateful coincidence"— that moment when you know what you are meant to do in this world.

She and Dr. Kosok worked together on a few papers. Eventually he moved on, but Maria dedicated the rest of her life to the Lines. Her stubbornness served her well. Not many other people would have embraced her difficult lifestyle. Maria didn't seem to mind. She said, "Even if I were sure that my blindness is due to the severe sun and all the limitations of my life on the plains, I would never have given up my studies."

Maria stands in the center of a spiral among the Nazca Lines.

Maria in 1932 in the countryside near Cuzco, Peru

Although Maria tried to be a rigorous scientist, she was also superstitious. When she first arrived in Peru, she had lost a finger to infection after exploring an Incan ruin. When she found the monkey figure, she was excited to see it had nine fingers, just like her. Maria looked at her hand and the monkey's and decided it was fate. She said, "The gods of these lands stole me when I was born. . . . That is why I am here."

Maria never sought fame or fortune, but she became famous as the Lady of the Lines, especially in her adopted country. In 1992 she was granted Peruvian citizenship. By this time Maria was revered by the entire nation, although she was frustrated by the attention. She said to a friend, "What good is it going to do me that they crowd me with honors, titles, and recognitions when I am already old, aged, blind, deaf and crippled? I want . . . the plains [to] be declared a national monument, so that the figures and lines do not get destroyed. I need this now and not later."

Who Were the Nazca People?

The Nazca lived in the river valley next to the Nazca desert from 500 BCE to 500 CE. They had no written language, so we study them from what they left behind. From their pottery, we know they took walks together and loved to dance. Their woven clothes (preserved by the dry air) show us they enjoyed bright colors. They were very clever about water: their aqueducts are reached by beautiful spiraling paths descending to where the water was under the ground. This spiral is repeated many times in the desert lines, once as the mischievous monkey's tail.

How Were the Lines and Figures Made?

The Lines did not require special technology to make. They were carved into the desert by scraping away the darker rocks on the surface and revealing the pale yellow soil underneath. The Nazca needed only simple tools and a good sense of geometry. Maria had a theory about how they might have enlarged a small design to an enormous one with string and pegs. Creating a geoglyph (the term for a large design carved into the ground) did not require a lot of time. An archaeologist and his team replicated the design and carving of the condor with only six people over two days.

Cat geoglyph discovered in the Nazca desert in 2020.

Who Discovered the Nazca Lines?

Maria was not the first to find the Lines. People had been noticing the curious scratches for centuries. Spanish chroniclers noted the Lines in the 16th century. The Peruvian archaeologist Toribio Mejia Xesspe noticed them in the 1920s and presented his findings to an archaeological conference in 1939. Dr. Kosok, the American anthropologist who first showed Maria the Lines, also studied them and published papers (some with Maria). Maria's invaluable contribution was her persistent study and protection of the Lines. Over four decades, she uncovered eighteen distinct figures and over one thousand Lines.

What's Happening Now?

New Lines are being discovered all the time. Satellite photography, drones, and artificial intelligence help archaeologists find new figures. Sometimes the figures are hiding in plain sight like the 120-foot-long cat found on a hillside in December 2020. The cat had been napping next to a staircase for viewing the Lines but was never noticed.

What Happens Next?

The Lines have lasted this long because the Nazca desert exists in a uniquely dry climate. The Humboldt Current, just off the coast, carries cold water from Antarctica to South America, cooling the air and keeping rain from forming. The rocks in the desert have baked into place under the hot sun. Without rain to wash them away, they have survived. However, rising water temperatures have led to more rainfall in Nazca, which could destroy the Lines.

Humans pose just as great a threat. In the 1930s, the builders of the Pan-American Highway never even noticed the lizard geoglyph as they cut it in half.

The Lines are now protected by UNESCO (The United Nations Educational, Scientific and Cultural Organization) but they are not safe. Careless trespassers scuff the Lines all the time. In 2014, Greenpeace snuck into the desert at night to erect a banner alerting world leaders about climate change. They filmed the publicity stunt and you can hear their sneakers crunching on the desert floor—damaging Lines and leaving permanent tracks—exactly what Maria feared.

What Was the Purpose of the Lines?

We don't know! Experts believe the purpose of the Lines may have changed over time. The figures (spider, monkey, tree, etc.) came before the straight Lines and geometric shapes. One theory is that the figures were meant as giant artworks to please the gods who flew overhead. The Lines and enormous trapezoids were carved later and often overlap each other, implying that they were not planned. We know from excavations that crowds gathered in the trapezoids, perhaps to celebrate religious ceremonies.

In 1968 a popular book *Chariots of the Gods?* claimed the Nazca Lines were ancient alien runways. Scientists laughed, but the book made Nazca a popular tourist destination (much to Maria's chagrin). When asked about aliens, Maria answered very seriously. Noting the softness of the ground beneath the Lines, she said, "I'm afraid the spacemen would have gotten stuck."

See for Yourself

Maria had to climb towers or fly overhead to see the Nazca Lines, but you can just go to Google Earth. Search "Nazca Lines" or "Nazca Spider" (or any of the other figures) and prepare to be amazed.

Maria takes measurements, 1942.

Timeline

500 BCE The Nazca people settle in the river valleys along the Nazca desert.

500 BCE–500 CE The Nazca begin carving shapes and figures into the desert. Archaeologists believe that the figures came first.

1537 CE The Spanish chronicler Pedro de Cieza de León visits the region of Nazca and notes the Lines, writing, "Signs in a part of the desert . . . so the Indians (Natives) can detect the way they have to follow."

1554 Spaniard Francisco Hernández Girón writes, "The Indians draw big lines in the soil."

1839 Don José María Córdova, a government official, notes, "In the neighbouring plains there are drawn many drawings in different figures."

1903 Maria is born in Dresden, Germany.

1927 Peruvian archaeologist Toribio Mejia Xesspe notices the Lines and calls them sacred pathways.

1932 Maria moves to Peru to work as a nanny.

1941 Dr. Kosok introduces Maria to the Lines. She agrees to work for him. Her trip to the desert is delayed by travel restrictions on foreigners during World War II.

1946 Maria moves to the desert and finds the spider.

1948 Maria first sees the Lines from a small plane.

1949 *Mystery on the Desert* is published.

1952 Maria discovers the monkey.

1954 Maria straps herself to a helicopter to make a map.

1955 Maria convinces the Peruvian Chamber of Deputies to protect the Lines.

1968 The second edition of *Mystery on the Desert* is published.

1976 At her own expense, Maria builds the viewing platform.

1992 Maria is awarded Peruvian nationality.

1994 UNESCO designates the Nazca Lines a World Heritage Site.

1998 Maria dies from ovarian cancer.

2018 Google honors Maria with a Doodle on the 115th anniversary of her birth.

Maria looks for lines in Nazca.

Selected Bibliography

The quotations used in this book can be found in the following sources marked with an asterisk (*).

(The spellings *Nazca* and *Nasca* are used interchangeably.)

*Bridges, Marilyn. *Markings: Aerial Views of Sacred Landscapes*. Essays by Maria Reiche. New York: Aperture, 1986.

*DM Hoteles Nasca. Plaque dedicated to Maria Reiche.

*Gameros Castillo, Wilfredo. *Maria Reiche*. Yo Publico, 2017. perlego.com/book/1872170/mara-reiche-english-edition-pdf.

Greshko, Michael. "Massive Ancient Drawings Found in Peruvian Desert." *National Geographic*, April 5, 2018. nationalgeographic.com/science/article/new-nasca-nazca-lines-discovery-peru-archaeology.

Hall, Stephen S. "Spirits in the Sand." *National Geographic*, March 2010. nationalgeographic.com/magazine/article/nasca-lines-peru.

*McIntyre, Loren. "Mystery of the Ancient Nazca Lines." *National Geographic*, May 1975.

Mendoza, Ann Maria Cogorno. "The Nazca Lines: A Life's Work." World History Encyclopedia. Last modified June 04, 2019. worldhistory.org/article/1395/the-nazca-lines-a-lifes-work/.

*Morrison, Tony. *The Mystery of the Nazca Lines*. Foreword by Maria Reiche. Woodbridge, Suffolk, England: Nonesuch Expeditions, 1987.

Nova. "Nazca Desert Mystery." Season 49, episode 14, "Nazca Desert Mystery." November 2, 2022. pbs.org/wgbh/nova/video/nazca-desert-mystery/.

*Palomino, Michael. *Maria Reiche from Nazca: A Life for the World*. Booklet of Province Administration of Nasca in celebration of 100th anniversary of Maria Reiche, 2003.

Reiche, Maria. *Mystery on the Desert: A Study of the Ancient Figures and Strange Delineated Surface Seen from the Air Near Nazca, Peru*. Lima, Peru: 1949. Reissued 1968.

*Schulze, Dietrich, and Viola Zetzsche. *Bilderbuch der Wüste: Maria Reiche und die Bodenzeichnungen von Nasca*. Halle, Mitteldeutscher Verlag, 2014. (Translated for the author from German by Reine Knorr.)

UNESCO World Heritage Convention. "Lines and Geoglyphs of Nasca and Palpa." whc.unesco.org/en/list/700/.

To Learn More

Daily Planet. "Exploring Peru Geoglyphs with Drones." Discovery Canada. May 3, 2018. youtube.com/watch?v=P8vOnFV6gpQ.

Digging for the Truth. Season 1, episode 10, "Secret of the Nazca Lines." History Channel. March 21, 2005.

Golomb, Jason. "Why The Nasca Lines Are Among Peru's Greatest Mysteries." *National Geographic*. nationalgeographic.com/history/article/nasca-lines.

Google Doodle. "Maria Reiche's 115lh Birthday." May 15, 2018. google.com/doodles/maria-reiches-115th-birthday.

Guardian. "Greenpeace Activists' Nazca Lines stunt angers Peruvian government." December 10, 2014. theguardian.com/environment/video/2014/dec/10/peru-greenpeace-nazca-lines-stunt-government-video.

Yanes, Javier. "Maria Reiche and the Technology Behind the Nazca Lines." BBVA Open Minds, May 16, 2019. bbvaopenmind.com/en/science/leading-figures/maria-reiche-and-the-technology-behind-the-nazca-lines/.

Acknowledgments

Special thanks to Ann Maria Cogorno Mendoza of the Maria Reiche Institute in Nazca, Peru, and Marion Morrison of Nonesuch Expeditions of Suffolk, England.

To Sari, Christine, Karen, and Krista—
who now know Maria as well as I do
—MM

For Dr. Manuel Chavarri, my father
and most dedicated person I know
—EC

Picture Credits
© Private Archive of Maria Reiche: 34; © Private Archive of Maria Reiche and South American Pictures/Maria Reiche Collection: 35, 37, 38, 40; © AFP Photo/Peruvian Ministry of Culture: 36

Text copyright © 2025 by Michaela MacColl
Illustrations copyright © 2025 by Elisa Chavarri
All rights reserved. Copying or digitizing this book for storage, display, or distribution in any other medium is strictly prohibited.

For information about permission to reproduce selections from this book, please contact permissions@astrapublishinghouse.com.

Astra Young Readers
An imprint of Astra Books for Young Readers,
a division of Astra Publishing House
astrapublishinghouse.com
Printed in China

ISBN: 978-1-6626-2009-6 (hc)
ISBN: 978-1-6626-2010-2 (eBook)
Library of Congress Control Number: 2024932083

First edition

10 9 8 7 6 5 4 3 2 1

Design by Barbara Grzeslo
The text is set in ITC Avant Garde Gothic Medium.
The illustrations are painted in acrylic gouache.

Maria goes higher on a ladder for a better view.